PAGAN VIRTUES

ALSO BY STEPHEN DUNN

PAGAN VIRTUES

⇒ POEMS ⇐

STEPHEN DUNN

W. W. NORTON & COMPANY
Independent Publishers Since 1923

For information about permission to reproduce selections from this book, write to
Permissions, W. W. Norton & Company, Inc., 500 Fifth Avenue, New York, NY 10110

For information about special discounts for bulk purchases, please contact
W. W. Norton Special Sales at specialsales@wwnorton.com or 800-233-4830

Manufacturing by LSC Communications, Harrisonburg
Book design by Chris Welch
Production manager: Lauren Abbate

Library of Congress Cataloging-in-Publication Data

Names: Dunn, Stephen, date– author.
Title: Pagan virtues : poems / Stephen Dunn.
Description: First edition. | New York, NY : W. W. Norton & Company, [2020]
Identifiers: LCCN 2019027097 | ISBN 9781324002314 (hardcover) | ISBN 9781324002321 (epub)
Classification: LCC PS3554.U49 A6 2020 | DDC 811/.54—dc23
LC record available at https://lccn.loc.gov/2019027097

W. W. Norton & Company, Inc., 500 Fifth Avenue, New York, N.Y. 10110
www.wwnorton.com

W. W. Norton & Company Ltd., 15 Carlisle Street, London W1D 3BS

1 2 3 4 5 6 7 8 9 0

FOR SAM TOPEROFF

An actually existent fly is more important than a possibly existent angel!

—RALPH WALDO EMERSON

CONTENTS

2

3

4

THE MRS. CAVENDISH POEMS

PAGAN VIRTUES

A POSTMORTEM GUIDE (1)

For my eulogist, in advance

Do not praise me for my exceptional serenity.
Can't you see I've turned away
from the large excitements,
and have accepted all the troubles?

Go down to the old cemetery; you'll see
there's nothing definitive to be said.
The dead once were all kinds—
boundary breakers and scalawags,
martyrs of the flesh, and so many
dumb bunnies of duty, unbearably nice.

I've been a little of each.

And, please, resist the temptation
of speaking about virtue.
The seldom-tempted are too fond
of that word, the small-
spirited, the unburdened.
Know that I've admired in others
only the fraught straining
to be good.

Adam's my man and Eve's not to blame.
He bit in; it made no sense to stop.

Still, for accuracy's sake you might say
I often stopped,
that I rarely went as far as I dreamed.

And since you know my hardships,
understand they're mere bump and setback
against history's horror.
Remind those seated, perhaps weeping,
how obscene it is
for some of us to complain.

Tell them I had second chances.
I knew joy.
I was burned by books early
and kept sidling up to the flame.

Tell them that at the end I had no need
for God, who'd become just a story
I once loved, one of many
with concealments and late-night rescues,
high sentence and pomp. The truth is

I learned to live without hope
as well as I could, almost happily,
in the despoiled and radiant now.

You who are one of them, say that I loved
my companions most of all.
In all sincerity, say that they provided
a better way to be alone.

1999

1

They let me help set up the tents, clean up
after the elephants.
Anything they wanted me to do, I did.

The sword swallower and the man who ate fire
were finicky about their props,
and I made sure everything was in place.

Kid, they said, if things aren't perfect,
illusion won't work.
I was content to observe, note how much

of it was practice, attention to detail.
Come mornings,
after bringing coffee to the barker,

I'd go to the big tent where the aerialists
were getting ready
to make sure what was difficult looked easy.

They'd rehearse falling and being saved.
But mostly they practiced
swinging into the hands of their father,

a terrible man whenever his feet
were on the ground,
but in the air a figure of strength and grace.

And one night there was the lion tamer
weeping drunk,
snapping his whip at nothing. And once,

after a day of catcalls and insults, I watched
the bearded lady
walking to her trailer with a razor.

The elephants swished their tails
when they saw me.
They swirled their powerful trunks.

By summer's end I was sure that they, too,
had had enough,
were just this close to running amok.

AFTER EXPERIENCE

Dusk in the valley, the inner weather of our nation
dimming, oh once I believed we could just flick on
some lights and behave as if we had another chance
at living a noon-life, as if light wouldn't expose
the barbaric as well as what might save us.

Now, my darling, I'd like to try to outlive
some of my vulgar passions, like optimism.
Let's together place a circle of candles
in a darkening field, and leave them unlit.
Let's begin to dance just for the sake of dancing.

ORIGINS

Let's say it was morning here in the east,
the moon still out, time not invented yet,
and I emerged from my cave
with a club and a slingshot in search
of breakfast, which was any fleshy thing
I could bring home. A man had a job
to do, as did the woman who soon
would be carving the success
of the hunt on the cave wall, and no,
we wouldn't call it making love, she'd
just bend over and I'd want to stick my thing
into her thing, though maybe we'd wait
until we both had bitten into the nameless
creature I'd split in two. It would be one
of the first fucks of mutual gratitude,
soon to become part of our dailiness.
Before long I wouldn't need
to kill a thing, or she to etch the pursuit
of hunter and hunted into the walls.
It became what we wanted to do all day,
every day, sometimes like an offering to a new-
found god, sometimes ordinary, like a snack.

I WAS THINKING

in the narrow confines of a single page
perhaps even of a single life,
the made-up can rival the likely,

the way fantastic things can enliven
and expand the possible, but it wasn't long
before I realized I was sounding like a man

I didn't want to be, who wanted to enlarge
and accumulate, deny that the elephant
he had made out of the labor of others

wasn't present in the room. I was thinking
we needed something like a moral GPS
that would guide us past the ridiculous

obstacles bound to get in the way,
a travel-through-your-life self-help book
that might show us how to get

where we need to be. I was thinking
of a story I wanted to believe—an ambivalent,
midlife story, hilarious and sad—

a man I knew arriving at a house
he thought was forever hers and his,
and finding there a goodbye note taped to the door.

Who then wouldn't need something
to guide him through the coming days?
Perhaps a story in which he was better off

without her? Or a tale I'd want for myself,
questionable yet true, the blame
equally distributed over a lifetime?

Whether he's a liar, seeker, or a man
on the moon with a telescope and a dream,
I'd want him to be part of an event

that never happened, but was repeated
enough that it might become plausible,
like a Lazarus rising from the dead,

or a virgin giving birth
to someone who would choose to die for us.
I was thinking America needed a miracle.

May 2017

NOTHING WILL WARN YOU

Nothing will warn you,
not even the promise of severe weather
or the threats of neighbors muttered
under their breath, unheard by the sonar

in you that no longer functions.
You'll be expecting blue skies, perhaps
a picnic at which you'll be anticipating
a reward for being the best handler

of raw meat in a county known
for its per capita cases of salmonella.
You'll have no memory of those women
with old grievances nor will you guess

that small bulge in one of their purses
could be a derringer. You'll be opening
a cold one, thinking this is the life,
this is the very life I've always wanted.

Nothing will warn you,
no one will blurt out that this picnic
is no picnic, the clouds in the west
will be darkly billowing toward you,

and you will not hear your neighbors'
conspiratorial whispers. You'll be
readying yourself to tell the joke
no one has ever laughed at, the joke

someone would have told you by now
is only funny if told on yourself, but no one
has ever liked you enough to say so.
Even your wife never warned you.

As insects go, lacewings seem to have nothing to catapult
them into significance, most of the time just showing off
for the centipedes and sawflies. I imagine they envy
wasps their ability to make a house for themselves,
and boll weevils their cottony usefulness. It seems
lacewings have nothing to do but be beautiful,
and so are dangerous. I've known a few
of their human counterparts, and have been fooled
by their slender bodies, the golden alertness
of their eyes, and for a while have forgiven a meanness,
even a cruelty, at their core.
                    Lacewings suck the bodily fluids
of aphids and other soft-bodied creatures,
and devour their unhatched eggs. I suppose cruelty
has an evolutionary purpose, but whatever it is
I've learned to be wary of little pretty things
that exhibit it.
                    I can see some perverse nobility
in the Asian tiger mosquito that needs nothing
more than a dab of blood from a few of us
before it lays itself down to die. And the behavior
of the praying mantis after sex has become part
of the inhuman comedy. I hear that in some cultures
lacewings are called stink flies because of an odor

they emit to deter enemies. I don't know who
or what these enemies are, but I hope enough exist
to save this world from creatures that stink and murder
and look graceful, gorgeous even, in the doing.

THE YEAR BEFORE THE ELECTION

It was a time when all the poets
seemed to be dying, my favorites
and a few I couldn't bear.
I folded back everything I knew
into everything I thought I knew
until I was a man living in a world
of his own crazy postponements.
The weather there was calm,
then tempestuous, then calm again,
an inner weather I felt at the mercy of.
A good friend dropped out of my life
without explanation, wouldn't answer
my letters or phone calls. A woman
wrote to me saying she was sorry;
I had no idea who she was.
Only a few of the now-dead poets
committed suicide, or drank themselves
into oblivion. Their deaths were blamed
on natural causes. What could be stranger?
A prolonged silence began. In the past
that might have meant an important conversation
was about to occur. It had, I was told,
but hardly any of us were ready to hear it.

THAT AUTUMN

That autumn, in and around the city known for its food
and its art, I couldn't decide between the apples
that had not yet fallen and the ones
in the Uffizi, beautifully still and inedible.
Would it be better, I wondered, to allow
the ones in the meadow a natural death,
or speed up the process by reaching
as high as I could for my pleasure?
Hunger, aesthetics—that autumn I'd try
to give myself a reason for one or the other
as if desire were explicable. True,
in the museum sometimes the apples
looked more delicious than apples could be.
I ate them with my eyes, felt them given to me
by he who made them, lovely bruised gifts
on a white plate. And, also true, in the meadow
outside of the city, I remember wishing
I had someone to thank for what was so reachable.
That wish is always with me, then disappears.

THE LAST HOUR

It was the last hour of what was left of day,
   dusk slowly darkening
what had been forest
   but now was only a scattering
of trees thinned out for profit.
   The lumbermen had come
with their saws and trucks, taking
   what they owned. Who could blame them
except perhaps a city boy like me?
   I knew it wasn't fair
to liken them to those who destroyed
   sacred monuments, but I wasn't
feeling fair. I had moved from Lex and 3rd
   to this mountainous nowhere
for the love of a woman. She was a naturalist,
   which didn't figure in the largeness
of my feelings. The forest that scaffolded
   her property was just bare branches
in winter; in other seasons greenery
   not nearly as beautiful as she.
But I found myself admiring those trees
   for the ice and wind and all
they had to face and withstand.
   And when the men drove off
without regard for what mattered
   to her and now to me,

I wanted to slash their tires, get in the way
    of whatever destination they believed
was theirs. Because I desired things
    to stay as they were
I knew they had to change. One of those
    controlled burns for the purpose
of growth might be necessary, or perhaps
    just something as irrational as love.

THE UNDERCOVER MAN

Before the normal barriers
get erected, and silence
takes on a texture,
and our secrets grow

like mold in a basement,
I want you to know I believe
in the kind of transparency
that gets me what I want.

Why would I tell you this?
Because women like you
find even a semblance of honesty
irresistible. I will listen with what

appears to be intense interest
to everything you say.
I'll look into your eyes
as if they contained

something vaguely coral
and deep. I'm the kind of man
who will not touch you
without permission, ostensibly

considerate, terribly polite
in public. At some point
you'll take my hand and place it
where it will feel especially invited.

Or you won't. It doesn't matter;
what I love are the preliminaries,
the seeing what, the great if.
Your wise friends are likely to warn

you about me. But you won't listen
because you'll recognize I'm the mask
behind the face, as close to the truth
as you're likely to get.

HISTORICALLY SPEAKING

It was a year of pirates in speedboats,
anonymous bullies spreading privacies
on the internet, and the worst of them
doing worse than that and wishing to be known
for what they'd done, their perfidy
an advertisement for a cause.

Thus it was a bad year for historians,
whose stories couldn't be correct
for longer than a few days. More than ever
the failures of memory
would combine with the slipperiness
of observation to produce versions
only people stuck in some ideology
could agree with.

It was a war
where the enemy sometimes was wearing
the same clothes as their opponents,
and both sides believed their cause
was righteous, and years from now the victors,
if we were unlucky, would tell it as it wasn't,

unless we were the victors, and our historians
would tell it from so many angles
that both *was* and *wasn't*
would read like a symphony of discordancies,
an honoring of so many counterpoints
that I, for one, might find it impossible to rest,
historically speaking, among all the bloodshed,
the horror, which would stop for a while and continue.

OFFICE PRAYER

If you enter, comrade, the world
of self-deception, as some of us consciously
have, you will need to come to terms
with the language of gossip and memos,
the interoffice chatter that dulls us,
severs the synapses, shuts out pity.
I say comrade because I wish to further
close the gap between the man
I once was and the man for years now
I've been trying to be. Not a communist,
but someone who's come to love money
for the many sweetnesses it can buy.
Oh Appearance, god of the office,
when you hear me begin to speak,
try to allow some room for the unspeakable
to have its say. Give us the gift
of insurrection. Bless the sudden flood
that teaches us to swim. Amen.

2

THE WOMAN IN THE BLUE DRESS

1

What is said about the woman
in the blue dress attracts and worries him.
There is strength in her fragility,
her former lovers say, a fearlessness.
He thinks it would be terrifying
to be in love with her. They say she would
know your secrets before you knew
they were secrets. She would name
your desires, and allow them
their freedoms. She would allow
her heart to break in front of you,
then finish a sentence that had
no clear destination, a sentence
that would find its thinking
as it went, searching for the origins
of its sadness. It would affirm
the worst of you, lament your virtues.
It would confound you, her fragile power
to live with contradiction. You'd want
to be better than you are, or could be.
You'd fail her, and she'd blame it
on being human, on being an animal
as she was. She'd laugh at your apologies.
She'd say betrayal is what occurs

long before any manifestation of it,
shortly after a first promise. She'd
acknowledge her guilt in the matter;
she'd remind you that loving
is an achievement, a constancy of renewal.

2

The man who says no
is someone who leaves a small trace
of where he's been, and what he's done,
invisible unless seen by someone
like the woman in the blue dress, blessed
with her kind of attentiveness.
The man has made a career of absence.
He counts the meetings he's missed,
the secret pacts he's made with the devils
of duty and responsibility, he counts them
among his freedoms. He loves the no
of irreverence, the no of never-
in-my-house, the no of no-tolerance
for ideas held by people he despises,
cocksure and sometimes even correct,
but fundamentally wrong, he's sure,
except as understood by that woman

in blue whose heart seems always divided
between revolt and acceptance.
She knows where such men have been
and what they've done, and what they
haven't, and forgives them for half of it.
He doesn't want to know her politics,
or her thoughts about religion,
though he's sure she has them.
The man who says no doesn't want
a reason this time to say no.
He's content that she might be a yes
on the other side of his tendencies.

3

It seems to him that other women
are always nearby, always asking
to be watched, spoken to.
He remembers traveling alone in Italy,
and seeing someone lovely sunning herself
on a balcony adjacent to his. Only a little wall
and a few large plants separate them.
She's topless, but after a while that doesn't matter.
She's reading a book he has written.
He can see her lips moving to some of the words.

When she wets thumb and index finger
to turn a page, he almost gasps. The woman,
he concludes, knows that he's watching her.
But the fact is—he'll learn this later—
she doesn't know. She's propped herself
on her elbows, smiling at something he's written.
"What is pleasing you?" he's tempted to ask,
but chooses instead to imagine it's the scene
in which the protagonist feels she's a prisoner
of her own taste. He goes back into his room
and writes a note, which he gives to the concierge.
"For the Woman in Room 408" it says, and he begins
to worry about the disappointments of the actual.

4

The other woman says yes when they meet
in the lobby. She says yes when he suggests
they go to a café. It's just the two of them.
It's all parry now, no thrust. The waiters observe
with bemusement what to them is historical.
Outside, waiting to be seated: Illness, Boredom, Sorrow.
Loneliness already seated, dining with a group.
For the man and the woman not much

of an investment yet. Their currency disposable:
hope and charm. Layers of it before their hearts
will be exposed. Their souls not in the vicinity.
A tilt of the head, a puffing up, this little dance—
they could be goats or birds. The future occurring.
The act of moving into it while keeping it at bay.
Between them, the unknown almost palpable now.
Look, Sorrow's just been let in, and given its favorite
table at the far end of the room. It's taking off its cloak,
slowly removing its disguise. It's Boredom in drag.
None of the waiters seem surprised.

5

Which is probably why he can't stop thinking
of the woman back home in her blue dress,
and how interesting he'd have to be all the time.
But what can a man do who is falling hard
except keep falling? On cloudy days,
like this one, the sun just peeking through,
the man who no longer wants to say no
envisions living with an irresistible radiance,
which won't be domesticated, offers no
instructions for how it can be endured.

Is the woman in the blue dress replaceable?
She'd be the first to say *Yes, of course.*
She might also say there'd be a cost,
and his task would be to discover
what would be left after she's gone.
Emotional bankruptcy? A one-way ticket
home to Mom? He refuses to think about it.

6

The man who says no wants to coax
and be coaxed. He laments what has happened
to the art of flirting, how rules are now posted
for it at certain businesses and universities.
"May I?" and "When?"—words that stop
the hands from where hands wish to go,
halt the great interplay of give and take.
What the man who says no
loves about the dress the woman is wearing
is that it isn't slit up the side,
doesn't tempt him with some deep V
of a neckline. It's her modesty that quickens
the moment, obviates the need for language.
He wants to break some rules, suggest she slip
into something darker, more thoughtful.

Wait, he can imagine her thinking,
let's wait until we can't wait any longer.

7

Her former lovers say
that with her there's no end to ambiguity.
Just when everything seems clear between you,
she says something wonderfully odd
like she's been watching a spider mend its web,
or that there's something to be learned
about architecture from the swoops of a swallow.
What can he say? Certainly not no.
But when she says there's a speakable grace
in the fields and even in the cities,
the man who used to just say no wants to say
something harsh, like "Don't you read the papers,
watch the six o'clock news?" But he can't,
because soon she's talking about the worn-out
husks of men and women returning from the factories,
the venereal streets, the bruise history
passes down to its forlorn children. Once again
she has him off balance. Now he can see her
in a T-shirt and overalls, though she's still
wearing that blue dress. Now he's more in love than ever.

8

Which is why he wants to tell her
what happened in Italy. He wants to come clean.
He says the weather was . . . He starts to speak
about the freshness of the food, a bottle of Barolo
he had one night in Venice . . . The truth is, he finally
says, I met someone lovely in many ways but not
the way you are lovely, someone who . . . but realizes
he's just skirting the surface. Sometimes, he says,
absence makes the heart grow sluggish,
and desire only one person, or else should we
just lean into life, inhale what we can of it?
Don't we all want what we shouldn't have?
She's smiling, which he chooses to think of as a sign
of agreement, as if a smile had only one meaning.

3

AN EDUCATION

For a while you believed
by putting just one phrase
on paper or a slash of paint
on a canvas—a gesture random
and accidental—that you were
on your way to the beginning

of an order. Or at the least
more of the world would be visible.
Maybe on lucky days
the arrival of some anxiety
or startling exaltation
could propel you beyond
the daily monotony, and there

it would be, the semblance
of what feels true.
Sometimes, though, you'd find
yourself making dazzling nonsense,
sometimes just plain good sense,
which might seem like wisdom
until everyone agreed with it.

THE FACE HE'S WORKING ON

The clown knows not to clown around
with other clowns. Flowers fade,
and often are beautiful—
about some things there are *ifs*,
about others the strangest certainties.
The funeral director has a fondness
for the embalmer's art, wants to know
if the dead should smile at the viewing,
wishes to please the living. Like the clown
he understands the happiness of others
is his job, can fake a tear if need be.
A flower has no obligations to anyone,
and even if it did lacks the capacity
to return to what it once was.
The clown never cracks a joke,
or blows up a balloon in private.
What others call beauty, the true artist
steps back from, adds some inappropriate
color to the face he's working on, enjoys
for a while the wildness of his addition,
then erases much of it, tries to hide evidence
of his labor. He knows that roses, six of them
in full bloom, hand-delivered, can't rival
one delicate moment of disclosure.
And yet he tries to reveal what serves
only what he's making, a just enoughness

that only sometimes is enough.
It's why clowns aren't good lovers,
always keeping too much of themselves
from themselves as well as from others.
And why the artist, even if he's needy,
isn't thinking of love while he's working;
he's happy if he can subvert at least one
opinion too tightly held by someone.

You shouldn't be surprised that the place
you always sought, and now have been given,
carries with it a certain disappointment.
Here you are, finally inside, and not a friend
in sight. The only gaiety that exists
is the gaiety you've brought with you,
and how little you had to bring.
The bougainvillea outside your front window,
like the gardener himself, has the look
of something that wants constant praise.
And the exposed wooden beams,
once a main attraction, now feel pretentious,
fit for someone other than you.
But it's yours now and you suspect
you'll be known by the paintings you hang,
the books you shelve, and no doubt
your need to speak about the wallpaper
as if it weren't your fault. Perhaps that's why
wherever you go these days
vanity has followed you like a clownish dog.
You're thinking that with a house like this
you should throw a big party and invite
a Nick Carraway and ask him to bring
your dream girl, and would he please also
referee the uncertainties of the night?
You're thinking that some fictional

characters can be better friends
than real friends can ever be.
For weeks now your dreams have been
offering you their fractured truths.
You don't know how to inhabit them yet,
and it might cost another fortune to find out.
Why not just try to settle in,
take your place, however undeserved,
among the fortunate? Why not trust
that almost everyone, even in
his own house, is a troubled guest?

THE ERRORS

The errors you've made and keep making
linger and indict you long after
they've become instructive. Just think
of the many times you've held doubt up
as a virtue, while knowing deep down
you were cocksure or believed otherwise.

The world is full of men like yourself,
masters of the apparently small statement
that balloons with hot air if not challenged.
You claim to have lived, for example,
among the daily varieties of injustice
without losing sight of what ought
to be done. Yet how often you were duped
by your own rhetoric, never really seeing
when things around you got ugly.

Now and then others step down
from their soapboxes and take to the streets,
confident their history-innocent solutions
can make a dent in what's wrong with us.
They are the doers, their collective errors
something to admire for their grit and panache
while your kind only dare to rage at home
or, in letters to the editor, merely complain.

PAGAN VIRTUES

If you have them, your day will overflow
with options; you can reexamine
everything that smells of dogma
or the forbidden, tip your hat
to the great poem that is the body,
maybe even uphold the beautiful

by renouncing the pretty.
Prepare to be in trouble on holidays,
which are holy days for others, but for you
are days off, a chance to exercise
your pleasures, perhaps speculate why prayer
never seems to reach its destination.

Tell your churchgoing friends
that you're more like a justice of the peace
than a witch or warlock, someone trying—
with the help of the best that's been written
and said, and without aid from the cloudy above—

to divine what's evil, investigate what's good,
attempt to live in a world a person from
another world might want to muck around in,
raise children, guide them to discover
for themselves what it means to be a citizen.

THE NORMAL

He wasn't surprised that his heart
would hit two opposing notes
at the same time. What could be
more normal? Sometimes he would
guess the superiority of one version
by the way the other told lies,
but mostly he'd live
with their coexistence, like his wish
to dominate and his love of giving in.
His abstract-painter friends would talk
about creating parallel universes.
His writer friends enlarged the world,
but made clear only some of it,
at best, was his to have.
A poker player once told him
her key to success was managing
to empathize with her opponents
while remaining devoid of all compassion.
For a while he thought that was a woman's truth;
then he went all in.

AS IF CHEKHOV HAD WRITTEN IT

After the final episode of The Americans,
a drama about Soviet spies posing as Americans

Chekhov with his cold eye would have
reminded us there's no escaping what we've done,
and therefore who we've become. But high up
on a hill overlooking a brightly lit Moscow
Philip and Elizabeth aren't sure, though we are,
how much disappointment awaits them.
Trained to be Americans, they've been found out,
and here they are in the sad country they've spied
and murdered for. Now we hear them speak
reassuring lies to each other: their children will be
okay, the world, the future. They believe everything
they've done has been for some larger good.
As if Chekhov had written it,
a sense of inevitability mixes with a sense
of doom, yet we feel a terrible tenderness
toward each of them, whom we've often despised.
It's 1988. In a year the wall will come down.
There's no escaping what we've been allowed to imagine.

A GOOD LIFE

Of course sadness, regret, even cruelty.
Of course the failures and the almosts.
It seems that time will undo everything,
though it's possible to be magnificent, too,
for days, even longer.
What can I do but risk the life
that flirts with fully being a life?
I haven't murdered anyone yet,
but have a list. I'm hoping my anger
will be offset by defiance.
If I'm honest I need to remember
to remember to be generous. The great
undoer, however, has patience on its side,
can outwait a fire in the forest.
The winning shot I made as a boy
has already slid into the reductions of memory.
I'll never be the same hero, and my teammates
never again as joyous as I want them to be.
And when it comes to her, my great love,
and our early sense of ecstasy, time will
likely be relaxing on the bed with us,
working the remote, choosing a comedy.

MISFORTUNE

When I woke after dozing on the patio, everything was silent.
A solitary buzzard rocked lazily in the sky.
I could smell misfortune coming on, literally smell it.
I knew it wasn't luck because I'd known luck
and its heartwarming scent of jasmine just blossoming.
And I knew it was different from unluckiness
which stinks up the air like pollution rising beautifully
from a smokestack. No, this smell was clean the way
rain that has yet to arrive smells clean. There was something
sharp in it, something that could damage and leave
little evidence. Many years have passed since I woke
on that patio with that foreboding murmur of silence
around me. It was then that I decided to keep to myself—
whatever it was—until life itself with its palpable
arrivals and odors would insist otherwise.
That is why you have found me laughing
when I trip and fall, emerging slightly bloody
and bruised, or when someone nearby and dear
complains too much about a nasty, persistent cold.
I still smell it, that clean, lingering scent of misfortune.
It's what keeps me alert, makes each new day bearable.

THE GHOST SONG OF THE RETIREE

Mornings after his usual eggs over easy
and in pursuit of someone kindred but gone,
he'd open the local paper to the obituaries,
noting what schools the dead had attended,
what positions they held and for how long.
Pitiful, he thought, how often he felt superior
or jealous. More and more he became aware
that his own past had ceased to exist,
but still trickled into each next moment.

Everywhere he went, he heard stories of retirees
apparently unburdened by self-consciousness
who could go entire days without worrying
about what had escaped them for years.
One might have a passion for gardening.
Another would combine a love to rebuild
with a fascination for destruction.
Still others were happy hobbyists, or tolerated
the occasional dreariness of travel or of home.

His wish was to use his newfound leisure
to enter the unvisited parts of himself.
He thought of it like some grand opening
of windows in a smoke-filled room.
That he mostly found loneliness and neglect
and some other empty places around the heart—

this was anticipated by those in charge.
They provided a ceremony for longtime service,
a watch, and a gold, embossed plaque
along with a few honest pats on the back.
What lay ahead for him was up to him, of course,
and couldn't be captured by camera or speech.
Over time he learned he'd need an astonishing array
of enthusiasms, and some deep fellow-feeling
just to barely hear the true rhythms of his elusive self.

The lies he succeeded in turning into achievements,
and the damning truths he couldn't escape
found their places in his personal museum
of embarrassments. Soon it was lunchtime
or walk-the-dog time, or time for him to once again
vainly interrogate some big *why* or *how come*.
He wasn't one of those retirees who knew the answers,
and he realized he only had a few more years
to plumb the mysterious and conjure a song
to some glorious unknown. He wanted the right words
to come to him, magically, that would work as well
as his regimen of pills. But he didn't want to bargain
with some keeper of them or yield to anyone
smarter than himself or have to offer good cheer.

Let's look at a day, any day, as it moves
toward nightfall, pleasure and catastrophe
occurring at somewhat normal intervals—
and let's design an instrument to measure the lives
we live, something perhaps with a bell that goes off
when we confuse playing-it-safe with maturity,
or common decency with heroism. And if
such an instrument fails because, once again,
the genius who can build it hasn't yet arrived
with the eloquence of a solution, let's acknowledge
most of us just let life happen to us, and how much
depends on the country and year we're born in,
and the varieties of abuse and love, poverty
and greed, that our parents and their parents
experienced and passed down to us.
Nor should we forget the quest for happiness
is rarely as strong as the quest for survival,
but when it is how interesting to discover
how far we'll go to attain the seldom attainable.
And let's instruct the historians among us
to include a chapter on Illusion, and maybe one on
Misunderstanding, and have them keep in mind
that most of our days are comprised
of card games, TV dramas, sex
or at least the thought of it, petty squabbles,
reconciliations—those little enormities.

4

THE MRS. CAVENDISH POEMS

RACHEL BECOMES MRS. CAVENDISH

She moved into his name
willingly, for reasons phonetically
and otherwise obvious.
She especially liked that Cavendish
had a ring of entitlement to it
among bankers and brokers
in the New Jersey suburbs
where they moved to escape
her friends and join his.
She was young, and had a sense
of what could be called Waspy fun.
She'd never met anyone like him.
Both of them kept me off-balance in those days.
When I'd visit I'd find myself half-beguiled,
half-annoyed, by how she'd tell lies
about things we'd experienced together.
But what could I do? She was in the act
of becoming Mrs. Cavendish, and I knew
from then on I'd keep her past
in the same closed-up closet
where I kept my own dark secrets.
In that way her husband and I became
keepers of her preferred memories.
He knew I loved her, but thought of me
as an adoring remnant, essentially prehistoric.
The truth is always different

from what anyone says out loud,
but who really cares? Not I, said the man
I chose to be, nor I nor I nor I—
among the many of us she left teetering.

THE YOUNG MRS. CAVENDISH

Because back then she accepted
almost any problem as the normal state of things,
she thought the homeless and the affluent
were just part of the landscape, inevitable as storms

and sunsets. It was easy, she said, such thinking,
and when it wasn't, it simply wasn't. I felt like
disavowing her right there, but I rarely knew
what to do in her presence,

found it hard to resist the lilt of her voice,
her blithe carelessness. When she began to use the word
spiritual as if it were something you could study for,
like citizenship, I should have collapsed into laughter.

Let's embrace our ignorance, I finally said to her,
half-aware I was revealing my own brand of sanctimony.
I remembered for both of us how pleased she was
when we discussed Ayn Rand and free enterprise,

and those years she instructed others in the art
of selfishness. Let the poor work harder,
she'd say, let the strong get stronger. She'd cite
Howard Roark as her man of the hour, would tell

anyone who'd listen that Adam Smith eats Marx
for breakfast. Then she went to college, and there
was the world, fraught with complications
of competing ideas. Now she says

she was an idiot, hadn't yet tripped over herself
in pursuit of an idea, or lost a job, or had to rely
on the kindness of the unambitious. It took forever
before she could separate the shit from the shinola.

HER LAMENT

She was good all day and did what she was supposed to.

Because she came to believe that everyone
has the right to be heard, but not necessarily
the right to be taken seriously, she was trusted
by all sides. And I, too, admired her,

but would argue that having so many friends
made her suspiciously indiscriminate.
"Well," she said, "I don't like you
very much, does that count?"

Taken aback, at the same time pleased,
I told her I was suspect too, an atheist
libertine coward, and often called my actions
mature when in fact I was playing things safe.

And this was how, after many years apart,
Mrs. Cavendish and I became friends again,
real friends, telling each other the semblance
of truth, always holding just enough back.

THE PERIOD OF MOURNING

Mr. Cavendish was William to his friends, Billy
to Rachel, a name she gave him in the sweet
early days of their courtship. After a few years,
things quieted into the various hums
of marriage. They spoke and suffered politely,
house and what-shall-we-have-for-dinner talk
replacing *baby, baby, oh baby*. By the time
Mr. Cavendish's car caromed off that guardrail
and spun into traffic, they had achieved the normal.

Nevertheless, Rachel mourned his absence,
now and then turning to me for something
to lean on, which I gave with a hidden gratitude.
For a long while I turned her sighs into stories,
yet welcomed when she started to laugh again,
freeing me from grieving what I had no heart for.
Mrs. Cavendish, I said to myself, I'm happy
and hopeful, but of course no one could hear me.

MRS. CAVENDISH'S DOG

I'm a dead dog for real now;
no longer can I rise
from my fakery, alert to commands
I'd come to think of as love,
though I never did obey
as well as Sundown did,
or as a truly good dog would.
To play the slave, not be one,
was my code. You understood,
who would play the master.
From my grave in the yard,
Mrs. Cavendish, I see now
you had no gift for it, or heart.
Bad dog, you'd say,
so little conviction in your voice.
In seconds you'd be patting my head.
Forgiveness made you happy; I'd tip
over trash cans to be forgiven by you.
Let me tell you it's no life being dead.
I'd give anything to chase the gulls again.
But clarities come when the body goes.
For whatever it's worth, you should know—
you who think so much—
only what's been smelled or felt
gets remembered. And in the dark earth
no doors open, no one ever comes home.

THE WINTER GUIDE

It's snowing, Mrs. Cavendish, maybe not just yet
where you are, but here it's coming down rabbits
and golf balls, and at this very moment a group
of tall albinos is convening on my lawn.
Let me be your hyperbolic winter guide,
and I'll have you forget what weathermen say
about worry and gloom. How about, for starters,
a long, defiant slide down Death Mountain,
everyone cheering you on? Or can we drive
to a mostly frozen lake, lace up,
and do figure eights where the soft spots are?
Or, if you prefer to stay inside, I'm a stay-inside guy
too. I like quiet games in which no one can lose.
It's snowing harder now, Mrs. Cavendish,
the wet and heavy kind. Even with my bad back
you should know I want to shovel your walk,
risk a spasmodic attack to be closer to your door.
The forecast is everything that's happening to me
will soon happen to you. Don't you like the way
that sounds? Think of it as the universe singing
my praises, all my mischief approved.
Mrs. Cavendish, it's blizzardy cold.
Come out anyway. Come out and play.
I've made a snowwoman dressed
in bright scarves and with charcoal eyes,
but clearly she won't do. She smells wrong,

so terribly clean. She's not you. From you
what I need is a sign. I have a key to the shed
where there's some wood and a wood-burning stove.
It's where we can dry off, change our clothes.

HER AMERICAN DILEMMA

Mrs. Cavendish, dear Mrs. Cavendish, I want
to say that though your husband was born
in England, you need not prove yourself American

by acquiring what you don't need. I've seen you
try to shop your way out of an impenetrable mood
at some cathedral of a mall, your small inheritance

dwindling day by day. I should rename you
Mrs. Conspicuous Consumption, she who
takes herself to the cleaners, and doesn't know

the cost. Prodigious, Mrs. Cavendish,
that's what you are. You told me once (in a weak
moment) you'd like to slow dance with me

to music only we could hear, inner melodies
so much ours you'd feel the beginnings
of something hard saying hello to your thigh.

That's all I think about now, a rising up
from almost nothing, my American dream.
Mrs. Cavendish, if it would please you

I'd lie down with you on one of those flat beds
that carries big merchandise at Home Depot,
then have someone roll us over to Walmart

or Staples, those giants that have swallowed
the little guys who once made the neighborhood
a neighborhood, and called me by name.

Maybe there's no connection between the demise
of Jack's Hardware and why so many hate us,
though I worry that to lie down with you

will activate those crazies on the lookout
for the likes of us, their backpacks
filled with motives and zeal.

I oppose and sympathize with their hatred,
but would be happy if a few of them
were hanged. It's so difficult to desire someone

and be principled, too. America the beautiful
some people sing, able to believe all the words.
Mrs. Cavendish, I'm trying. I'm trying for you.

Morning and the moon still out,
a gauzy moodiness over the land
as the sea struggles with the old
magnetism from above. Mrs. Cavendish,
the sea doesn't want to be bothered today,
it merely wishes to behave like a lake,
reflect back a face it believes is its own,
sometimes wild, mostly calm.
It also would like to change
its salty ways, but like you,
Mrs. Cavendish, it can't—

                   the world is various
but also cruel. I tell you, Mrs. Cavendish,
you should buy a big flat-screen TV and engage
the world in the safe way most of us do.
When the census man comes with his charts
and those categories he'll want you to check,
remember to lie about your age. Tell him
you're not happy about the end of secrecy,
you don't want to become a stat.

                        At another time
the sea, too, will want to undulate and roar,
not be lake-like at all. Mrs. Cavendish,
there's so much whim and peculiarity
to accommodate. I wish I could tell you
the best stroke to use if you choose to swim

where the orcas rule. All I know
is that you shouldn't answer if a man
without a heart asks about yours.
He'll have plans. They'll be for you.
And soon the moon will recede, can't help,
will only serve as witness, as the cosmos does.

MRS. CAVENDISH AND THE DANCER

Mrs. Cavendish desired the man in the fedora
who danced the tarantella without regard
for who might care. All her life she had
a weakness for abandon, and, when the music
stopped, for anyone who could turn a phrase.
The problem was Mrs. Cavendish wanted it all
to mean something in a world crazed and splattered
with the gook of apparent significance.
The dancer studied philosophy, she told me,
knew the difference between a sophist
and a sophomore, despite my insistence
that hardly any existed. It seemed that everyone
but she knew that sadness awaits the needy.
Mr. Cavendish, too, when he was alive,
could be equally naive, might invite a wolf
in man's clothing to spend a night
at their house. This was how she
mythologized her husband—a man of what
she called honor, no sense of marital danger,
scrupled beyond all scrupulosity.
The tarantella man was gorgeous and oily,
and, let's forgive her, Mrs. Cavendish
was lonely. His hair slicked back, he didn't
resemble her deceased in the slightest,
which in the half-light of memory's belittered
passageways made her gaga. And I, as ever,

would cajole and warn, hoping history
and friendship might be on my side.
Mrs. Cavendish, I'd implore, lie down
with this dandy if it feels good, but, please,
when he smells most of sweetness, get a grip,
develop a gripe, try to breathe your own air.

MRS. CAVENDISH AND THE GENERAL MALAISE

Like a boxer at a prefight weigh-in, defiant,
no sign of acceptance, Mrs. Cavendish began
to stare meaninglessness in the eye.
The difference: no one, nothing, stared back.
Mrs. Cavendish, I said, it's impossible to win.
As we consider today, it's almost tomorrow.
As we admire the flowers, how easily they're ravaged
by wind and rain. The best we can hope for
is a big, fat novel, slowing down the course of time.
Several tomorrows always linger in the margins,
which means until the very last page
you'll choose to live with the raw evidence
of how someone else sees and makes a world.
Mrs. Cavendish, I'm also sorry to report
the maps are missing from the office of
How to Get Where You Want to Go—
just one more symptom of the general malaise.
I have little hope that they can be found,
at least not in our lifetime. At the risk of telling you
what you already know, Mrs. Cavendish, here's
something merely true: the insufficiency of the moon
has been replaced by the lantern, the lantern by
the light bulb, but what won't go away is the promise
of salvation out there in the bright beyond.
There will always be people who think suffering
leads to enlightenment, who place themselves

on the verge of what's about to break, or go
dangerously wrong. Let's resist them
and their thinking, you and I. Let's not rush
toward that sure thing that awaits us,
which can dumb us into nonsense and pain.
My dog keeps one eye open when he sleeps.
My cat prefers your house where the mice are.
Stare ahead, my friend. The whole world is on alert.
Mrs. Cavendish, every day is old news.

MRS. CAVENDISH'S DREAM

I had spoken to her, she said, from some faraway
unidentifiable place, and I was all mouth,
three times the size of any mouth
she'd ever seen. It was a mouth that didn't want
to suck or kiss so the dream didn't seem sexual,
nor did it want to devour, thus she was not fearful.
The mouth only seemed to want to speak
and be heard, and right before she woke
she remembered thinking she wished it was an ear,
a giant ear that would encourage her to say and say
and say. The next day on the telephone,
she concluded the mouth had all the vatic
and pontifical qualities of a poet's mouth, and probably
was mine. Did it speak? I asked. And if it did,
what did it say?—always searching for giveaways
that might indicate what she thought of me.
*If you want to live in the wilderness, make sure
you know the difference between ordinary shit
and the scat of grizzlies,* is what the mouth said.
Then before she fell back to sleep, the mouth added
something like, *Let's return to zero.*
Mrs. Cavendish—I was laughing as I spoke—
I think you made that up. No, she said, it's all true,
except maybe the third "say," which was irresistible.

The cross-dresser, the albino, the man who once had legs,
and so many others out there displaying their otherness—
Mrs. Cavendish, how long it took us to recognize they want
what we want, and how they must struggle. Some are brave,
many just silly or stupid, as we have been, and stumble
into daylight like things that have always lived underground.
To wish to be loved, and not be able to see where you're going—
oh Mrs. Cavendish, you know what I'm talking about.
So difficult for us to exit the mirrorless rooms we grew up in.
So difficult to know the dark, brotherly other in ourselves.

I do know, however, it's easy to take a false step
by standing still, or to cling to a single identity.
But I'm not sure if I'm brave or deprived enough
to be an outlaw. Are you, Mrs. Cavendish?
Once I was asked to believe in a radiant goodness.
Had I been given another choice—something
that spoke to the life I lived—I might have a prayer
a bad boy could say with conviction. Mrs. Cavendish,
I don't. I can only imagine the words floating, unspoken.

MRS. CAVENDISH SPEAKS

Don't get me wrong, I'm occasionally grateful
for my friend's advice, but sometimes
he doesn't understand that the rational
separates this from that, leaves behind
more than it can combine or make sense of.
Truth is, I simply don't want
the world he wants. Give me the unfilled
space between hunger and the morsel
it can't quite reach, or between taste
and the aftertaste that's remembered
and therefore forever sought.
I want my sense of sense to be uncooperative,
the way the truly sensual self-interested is.
And while I'm complaining, I wish
he'd call me Rachel, as he did
in the old neighborhood
when he'd dribble his basketball
in front of my house to get my attention.
Maybe it's because I always give him
less than he craves that the formality
of Mrs. Cavendish exists between us.
Maybe he believed marriage changes who a person is.
And who knows, maybe it does and did.
I became Mrs. Cavendish to him,
perhaps because he needed that distance.
But after my husband died, I think I've become

Rachel again. I know quite well the follies
of the sensual are similar
to the follies of the logical,
and have learned to be wary of both.
Yet I want to say, Oh my dear friend,
just because I don't listen is no reason
for you to stop saying what you must.

Mrs. Cavendish was aware of the tick
of the clock, the seemingly often unseemly
progress of time, but knew little of the *now*,
which was known to go backward, or pick up
where it left off. We'd argue about such matters,
affectionately, because she knew I trusted her
mindful instincts, as much as I knew
she tolerated mine. Death shows no favoritism,
she once said, and added that history
was a strangely beautiful graveyard
where the rich lie down with the poor.
But in general Mrs. Cavendish
loved the enigmas of happenstance
more than any slippage toward certainty,
and the truth-teller in her loved
as if more than *this is so*.
It was easy to be fond of this person
she had become, her heart often ascending
to where her mind presided,
properly warming what got spoken.
I marveled at how she could disturb
wisdom with the gentlest of doubts,
but also worried that she couldn't commit
to any one thing. One evening I said,
Mrs. Cavendish, I'm afraid you need something

to give your whole self to, or maybe
some rules for getting to a place inescapable,
some place not in between.
How then would I stay alive? she said.

MRS. CAVENDISH SPEAKS OF THE UNFORGIVABLE

More than once I've permitted in myself
what I wouldn't forgive in others.

MRS. CAVENDISH RETURNS FROM INNER SPACE

She hardly knew she'd been gone, so familiar
and comfortably odd the atmosphere had seemed
to her. She'd been inhabiting herself, feeding off
of what she'd accumulated over the years—the sweet
and the bittersweet—in search of the real Cavendish.
She said she'd been in the land of whispers
and secrets, the sun now and then breaking through
cloud cover to form her particular universe,
sometimes fraught, sometimes serene.
Mrs. Cavendish, I said, I'm glad to have you back,
looking so svelte and ready for what
the world must still have in store for you.
She lived a while with the answers, she reported,
which questioned and doubted themselves,
everything temporary and fixed, then temporary again.
Nothing was in store for her, nothing at all.
And I, who had kept watch as she disappeared
and returned—often without moving a muscle—
wanted to say to her that here in the brightness
of her kitchen, among the unquestionable
silverware, the certainty of the four walls around us,
I was hurt a little but not surprised
that she seemed not to need—prematurely
I felt—what always I had given her.

MRS. CAVENDISH COMES TO TERMS

When she was alone, she said, everything and everyone—
the streets she walked, the people she passed,
even the birds in the trees—also seemed alone.
At home, she'd avoid mirrors and their keen accuracies,
        and once when I called on her she asked
what I saw when I turned the light on
in a darkened room, the dark illuminated or just less
of the dark? Were the bones of the room suddenly aglow?
        Mrs. Cavendish, I said, you sound depressed,
you should look for someone poorly trained—they abound—
and make an appointment without intention
of keeping it. In other words, be like me—
        a gesture toward, no actual fessing up.
I was pleased that she smiled, and took it as a sign
we were on the same blank page, had mutual ways
of fooling ourselves. Mrs. Cavendish, what shall we do
        if we can't have the fine loneliness lovers have,
their arms encircling what is so tentatively theirs?
Shall we kick some cans up and down the street,
fill the emptiness with cacophonous clangs?
Strange comforts are not what I want, she said.

Mrs. Cavendish, let's continue, out of habit, to expect
from death a tiny leniency, and when it arrives
let's see if we can choose the transport of our choice.
Not an airplane, of course, but something that might
descend at a speed slow enough to keep up
from what can spoil the illusion of a good time.
Maybe even a vehicle that doesn't move.

But let's not count on it.
Hope, Mrs. Cavendish, is a four-letter word.
Have a little fun, that's all. Wear your hair
in Medusa curls, and turn a few onlookers into stone.
Or like a caterpillar begin to undress, do a little
twirl and a shrug, and emerge as something else.
In the meantime, I'll stay around, an itch in my heart,
sleeping in a different room. Hope it. Hope it all.

MRS. CAVENDISH AND THE BEYOND

Beyond the mountain peak, a roundish glowing thing
was in some early stage of becoming itself, or was it
a helium-filled balloon on its way to a metropolis?

I couldn't tell, but we both saw it from her porch,
and uttered a collective *Look!* then got quiet
for a moment or two and just stared.

It's merely an alien ship from another world,
Mrs. Cavendish finally said, with the confidence
of a woman who'd gone far, albeit only in books,

toward expertise on such matters. As usual,
I was suspicious of what I called *easy mysticism*,
and wondered if it were a new schtick of hers,

or had she been, for years, following the advice
in the *I Ching* or from fortune cookies? I feared
she might be suffering from a case of innocence.

But suddenly the balloon or whatever it was
seemed threatening, as if it were about to descend
or explode in midair, moving as if out of control

or being controlled by a foreign force. Every machine
will break down at some point—I knew that—but is
also susceptible to tyranny, which made me think

about how many people might want to get back at us
for the use of bombs and drones in the name
of goodness and our way of life. Mrs. Cavendish, I said,

you're thinking interplanetary, and I hope you're right,
but international would be more worrisome, wouldn't it?
As far as I know, we haven't hurt anyone on the moon,

haven't taken out a village on Mars or Jupiter.
But just then the thing sped away
over the mountain, as if its mission was a desire

to become a memory, and had been completed.

THE DEMOCRACY GAME

We were watching television, my hand
on your thigh, and I wanted you to pay
special attention to that senator on the screen—
how good he was at voicing public outrage
at the deceit he'd mastered in back rooms.

See, I said, that's how the game is played;
you seek consensus, but only after
you've twisted the necessary arms.
I remember you looked at me strangely, as if
I were advocating instead of pointing out.

I went on to say, Mrs. Cavendish, it's not
that I approve. I love to watch the possible
take shape. And I love to see it defeated too.
Sometimes all it takes is the simple truth,
someone actually saying what he means.

What makes you think, she said,
that I don't understand move and counter-move,
or, now, where your hand wishes to go?
Isn't politics the art of getting what you want?
Think higher of me, my friend. Higher, please.

Evening becomes you, Mrs. Cavendish, because
that's when longing and possibility congeal,
become one, your black dress slit
up the side, and the cinematic way you glide
(in my mind) down long corridors
like that graceful woman in *Marienbad*—
only as I remember she was dressed in white,
diaphanous, her gait slow and apparently without
purpose, though at the end of one corridor is a man,
playing a game he can't lose, which other players
can't resist, and you're headed his way.
Someone is going to die, I'm going to make sure
not you, because this dream, this movie
is mine now, and I want to go as far as I can
into it, beyond any affirmation or certainty,
to a place where you can neither accept nor refuse,
you whom I ask once again to give up your name.

She would often seek that splendid rush,
not caring that it would soon subside.

After all, the issue was joy; she knew
it was never meant to last. Disappointment

was always nearby. She couldn't make
it disappear, or entirely ignore it,

but once she discovered the freedoms
within boundaries, it was like living

with a difficult but fair father, something
to push against while you found your own way.

Mrs. Cavendish, I said, I'm on your side. Like you,
I abhor the pretty good, the okay—those enemies

of wonderment. I want everything that's mine,
she said, to rise, be contained, spill over.

MRS. CAVENDISH BECOMES THE REAL THING

With the expectation of someone who has
succeeded more than once, Mrs. Cavendish
sits down each morning to engage the world.
Each day is a first day, and nothing is quite real
to her unless, finally, it bears her signature.
By the time she finishes breakfast, she's sure
that a well-made omelet falls under the category
of an intrinsic good, and is equally convinced
that the shape of a lemon is superior to that
of an orange—that beauty, if symmetrical,
is one of the enemies of improvisation.

She reads a little before she attempts a sentence
of her own, vows never to use the word *God*
because she's read that it's a word
that frightens God, makes Him go away.
But Mrs. Cavendish can't help but blaspheme
her own tenets, and, besides, believes a God
that isn't here can't be a God that goes away.
She writes, *Give me a steady authentic flame
that lights the way home,* and says it to me over the phone.

I tell her I love the line, but the fact is
the smarter Mrs. Cavendish gets the more I recede.
Even her silences bring news that is news
to me, a strange accuracy in the ways they shape
how I feel. Like now. Like sure-to-be tomorrow.

I don't know what else to say, except *hello
Mrs. Cavendish, hello from afar.*

THE MAN LEFT BEHIND

Without power, among the sunken skipped stones and shipwrecks,
I heard the wind taking ownership of the trees, and rowed
without purpose, neither weakened nor strengthened
by hope or despair. Last week, I could see beaver dams
upriver and other signs of natural trouble, but I pledged to keep
going, waterway after waterway, until you were found.

But of course, Mrs. Cavendish, you could be dead by now,
and the spot where your skiff went down
will never be known. But you could also be somewhere
hanging on, maybe to a log, waiting for me, or some sailor
in search of a mermaid you'd become if you could.
I've read about a lotus that survived

at the bottom of a lake for twelve hundred years,
then sprouted again, and coconuts that would float
across an ocean, wash ashore, and take root.
Maybe you're in a hotel room with the man who helped
you fake ruin. He's ordering from room service french toast
for two, blueberries and cream.

And your name, is it the same? And what do you want?
When someday you're discovered alive, I hope you'll find
this note I'm leaving at the dock with the old master of jibs
and slips who knew us when. He'll know where I am.
You see, I've thought of everything,
the way a man left behind does, Rachel my love.

A POSTMORTEM GUIDE (2)

Once again for my eulogist, in advance

You, too, are nineteen years older now,
and no doubt will say these roughly similar words
with a different sense of gravitas. I've changed,
but not as much as the world has.
I thought I had accepted all the troubles,
which is no longer true. And rage these days
has depleted that exceptional serenity
I once wanted you to claim I had.
Since you moved away we've hardly spoken,
and I'd understand if you feel you're now
the wrong man for the job. Back then
you were the only one who knew I had
an incurable disease. Well, no longer
can it be hidden. I stumble and fall,
shake and drool, but history's daily horror
trumps any condition of mine. What is it
compared to genocides and demagoguery?
There'll be fewer people at the service this time,
perhaps a few grandchildren, maybe even a few
others who've read a few of my poems.
Tell them it was true, I *did* think I'd die at sixty,
in my prime, in love with mystery and its words.
What I wished for you to say was sincere. Then
I met a woman who chose to marry me, a man
unguaranteed, a selfish man who said he'd give her
five years. Tell them it was she who bargained

for ten, then fifteen, and is holding out for more.
Tell them everyone needs a persuasive advocate
to forestall the oncoming desolations of the heart.
If there are tears then, trust that you have broken
through to where thoughts of me have let loose
in them thoughts of opportunities they've missed,
a splendor unlived. Steady your voice, and tell them
even if we've known despair it's possible
with some luck and some love to wander,
sometimes happily, in the despoiled and radiant now.
End that way, because the whole truth,
as I've tried to say before,
is nothing anyone has to know.

2018

Acknowledgments

APR: "A Good Life," "Office Prayer"

The American Journal of Poetry: "The Ghost Song of the Retiree"

The James Dickey Review: "Close to Running Amok" (originally "The Apprentice")

The Georgia Review: "That Autumn," "The Normal," "A Postmortem Guide" (1 & 2)

The Kenyon Review: "I Was Thinking," "Pagan Virtues"

New Letters: "Nothing Will Warn You"

The New Yorker: "The Inheritance"

The Paris Review: "Historically Speaking"

Plume: "The Face He's Working On"

Rattle: "Little Pretty Things"

Solstice: "The Undercover Man"

The Southern Review: "The Year Before the Election," "The Woman in the Blue Dress"

All of the Mrs. Cavendish poems were published, many with different titles, in *Keeper of Limits*, a chapbook from Sarabande.

My great thanks and love to my faithful readers and critics Lawrence Raab, Barbara Hurd, Sam Toperoff, and James Hollis, for their help with these poems. And a large thank you to Sarah Gorham for her generosity and permission to reprint the Cavendish poems.